Trust Your Gut

The Surgeon's Guide
to Getting It Done

by Tom Nicholson, MD, MBA
with Jen Singer

First published by Dog Ear Publishing
4011 Vincennes Rd
Indianapolis, IN 46268
www.dogearpublishing.net

ISBN: 978-1-4575-3812-4

This book is printed on acid-free paper.

Printed in the United States of America

Dedicated to my son Bobby Nicholson.

—Tom

For my brother, Scott, my entrepreneurial hero.

—Jen

Table of Contents

INTRODUCTION

"Gunshot. Surgical team to the ER. Stat."

A bullet wound is an unpredictable event. The only sure thing about it is that it'll do damage. Smaller-caliber bullets tend to tear organs and blood vessels and then bounce off bones, ricocheting in other directions to do more internal damage to muscles and tissues. Larger-caliber bullets rip through everything in their path.

A bullet's entry wound might be small and neat, but the exit wound can be a gaping tear the size of your fist. The path of the bullet—where it enters the body, if it meets any obstruction that causes it to change direction—affects the wound, the treatment, and whether or not I have a realistic chance of saving my patient's life.

A sixteenth-of-an-inch variation in the bullet's path can mean the difference between a victim living or dying, the difference between a family crying tears of gratitude or shedding tears of grieving agony when I meet with them in the waiting room.

Every single thing that a bullet damages has to be repaired.

Fast.

"Gunshot. Surgical team to the ER. Stat."

I look at my watch. Five seconds have passed since the first call for the surgical team, and already, my mind is playing an endless loop of images: every shooting victim I've ever treated, every outcome, good and bad, every blood vessel clamped and unclamped, every grieving mother, every tight-lipped father quivering with barely controlled emotion.

My feet are moving before I'm even aware that I've gotten up from behind my desk. As I head toward the ER, I join a growing stream of other doctors and nurses from the surgical team, all reacting to the same message that I heard.

"Gunshot. Surgical team to the ER. Stat."

"What's the ETA on the ambulance?"

"Single victim?"

"Do we know caliber? Number of bullets?"

I am almost at the ER when I realize that I'm the only one who's been asking these questions. Everyone else is grim and silent, ready, looking to me to make the decisions and take control of the situation.

I'm the surgeon, the chief of surgery. I'm in charge.

"Gunshot. Surgical team to the ER. Stat."

I arrive at the ER just as the paramedics are rushing the gurney from the ambulance into the trauma bay. I can see that the situation is dire. One paramedic is using a bag valve mask to ventilate the victim, and the dressings that the paramedics have applied are saturated with blood.

I am completely aware and focused on the situation. While I pull on my surgical gloves, my eyes are on the gurney being rolled into the OR. As the ER team coordinates the transfer of the victim from the gurney to the hospital trundle, the paramedic reports the status of the victim to me: "Unresponsive twenty-three-year-old male. Three gunshot wounds to the abdomen. Unknown caliber. No exit wounds. Pulse thready with a rate at one-forty. Blood pressure is extremely low, at eighty over forty-five. Blood oxygen saturation is decreased at 85 percent. You've got a large-gauge catheter in his left arm with intravenous saline running wide open."

"Intubated?" I ask.

The paramedic shakes her head. "No."

I already have a vast amount of information to assimilate. The victim is young—that's good news. Hopefully, it means that he was also healthy prior to the shooting, which will help him during surgery.

There are no exit wounds. That means there are three bullets somewhere in his body, three bullets that have danced around, doing all sorts of damage before coming to rest in an organ, alongside an organ, in fatty tissue … *somewhere.*

His blood pressure is dropping, and he's not oxygenating well.

This young man, who only moments ago was a shooting victim, is now a patient. *My patient.*

And he's dying.

What am I going to do?

But that's the wrong question. The right question is, "What am I going to do *first?*"

Everything I know about making good decisions (and making them fast), I learned in medical school, in my residency, and on the job as a surgeon. Well, maybe not *everything.* My dad taught me a lot about processing effectively and diagnosing quickly. As an interventional cardiologist, he knows how to weed out the zebras from the horses, how to assess the margins of error, and how to process pieces of information to arrive at the best solution for the situation quickly and efficiently.

Growing up, there was no room for mucking around in my high-energy, high-achieving family. You had to get to your point quickly and concisely or else lose the debate. And we sure had lively debates at the dinner table—about math, science, current events, and life in general. As a result, my brother (now a cardiologist), my sister (a malpractice attorney), and I were brainwashed—in a good way—to be efficient in our thinking and in our communicating. Get to the point and get to it quickly and efficiently, or else lose the floor to someone who has a better point that's more effectively presented.

What's more, my dad taught me that we shouldn't take one to two hours to do homework when we could do it in thirty minutes. That's right: My father wanted me to spend *less* time on my homework (but he still expected good grades). He is, after all, a man who can install heart catheters in two to three minutes as expeditiously as other doctors can in thirty. His model for efficiency has afforded me a thriving career and a well-rounded life.

While at Franklin & Marshall (where, by the way, my whole family attended college), I managed to double-major in premed and chemistry and also play basketball without feeling overwhelmed. As a surgeon, I've streamlined my practice so I can see a full caseload of patients and still have time to coach my son's baseball team and get out on the golf course several days a week, yet I'm not constantly dashing from one place to another, looking at my watch, and worrying about what I have to do next. In my family, we don't value busy-ness; we value efficiency, and surgery is all about efficiency, because once it's cut, it's cut.

Knowing how surgeons make decisions can help you make good ones, too. How we **diagnose**, **decide**, **do**, and finally, **discharge**, has applications beyond the OR, no matter what field you're in or what decision you need to make.

See, I'm constantly flummoxed by people who can't seem to arrive at decisions efficiently or effectively. Whether I'm seeing hospital administrators who get stuck in the diagnosis of the problem, residents caught up in making decisions based on clinical data alone, or friends who know what their problems are and how to fix them but fail to follow through, something in me screams, "Trust your gut!"

In this book, I boil down the surgeon's shortcuts to making good decisions, illustrating each part of the process with nonmedical anecdotes (House Calls) and supporting them with Gut Checks, practical advice based on a surgeon's field-tested decision-making principles. If you find yourself stuck in any one (or more than one) stage of decision making, this book will help get you unstuck, by providing a simple-to-follow, systematic, and heuristic (a system of experience-based mental shortcuts or rules of thumb) method for finding an efficient solution with the least potential error. And it works no matter the decision you're facing.

I'll take a close look at the four D's of surgery (diagnose, decide, do, and discharge), and I'll show you how they can relate to your own decisions. As I've learned in the OR, if there are errors in any one (or more) of these areas, the outcome can be anything from disappointing to devastating. Each of these four principles involves a web of experience, book smarts, street smarts, gut instincts, intuition, data crunching, and tried-and-true systems. Put them all together, and you can't help but make good decisions. I'll show you how.

Though the basic rules for surgery have been the same for the past hundred years, every patient, every appendix, and every gunshot wound are different. The way we surgeons make decisions is part education, part situation, part experience. It's intuition and gut instincts, checked against steadfast rules and yes, even flow charts. Any trained surgeon knows there's a host of decisions to be made— each of them important—before he or she decides where to cut. As a result, the surgeon's way of making good decisions can help guide you to make your own. Stat.

So, are you ready to scrub in?

(Oh, by the way, the patient above went home after five days in the hospital. But there were a lot of decisions made before he was discharged.)

PRINCIPLE ONE

DIAGNOSE

Sometimes I wish I could diagnose a patient based on just one symptom. It would certainly make my job much easier. But a stomachache can be caused by everything from strep throat to bad sushi to a tumor. To make an accurate diagnosis, I have to take into consideration all of the patient's symptoms, plus the medical and family health histories and the results from the physical exam and lab and imaging tests.

While I'm gathering all that information, I'll likely have a hunch about what the correct diagnosis will be. That hunch can either be spot on or way off, but I won't know for sure until all the information is in.

Sometimes, confirmation of a diagnosis doesn't happen until surgery, when suddenly, I'm staring inside a patient at peritonitis, a life-threatening inflammation of the tissue that lines the organs of the abdomen. Its most common symptom is severe abdominal pain—as it is for appendicitis, kidney stones, aortic aneurysm, the stomach flu, urinary tract infection, food poisoning, and mesenteric ischemia, which is a blockage in the arteries that supply blood to the intestines.

One symptom won't tell me all I need to know to make an accurate diagnosis, but it can send me on the right path. The chief complaint, or that main symptom that's causing the patient the most grief, can help me decide which other symptoms to check for and which tests to order. Yet I can head down that path only to have a test result send me back to the beginning to start over again.

Making the right diagnosis can feel like a game of Chutes and Ladders. Just when I've climbed up almost to the end, I slide back down toward the start. When you're trying to determine an accurate diagnosis, you have to be prepared to advance and fall back again. It's all part of the game.

DIAGNOSE

Rule One: Determine Just How Sick the Patient Is

You can't make decisions effectively or efficiently until you recognize how big or small the problem is and how fast or slow you have to move.

I wanted to be like George Clooney on *ER*. I wanted to make the big decisions, the ones that save lives. So after four years of college and another four in medical school, I entered the working world with a healthy sense of book smarts, a crisp white doctor's coat, and delusions of grandeur. When I reported for duty as a newly minted intern with the letters MD after my name for the first time, I felt ready to put into practice what I'd learned in textbooks, labs, and classrooms—only, the chief fellow in charge of my heart surgery rotation had other plans for me.

"Your job is to gather as much data as possible," he said. "And then find me, because I'm the one who knows how to use it."

Even after eight years of higher education, my role could pretty much be described as "information gatherer." I still had five years of my residency ahead of me, where I would learn how to add experience, intuition, and gut instincts to the foundation that my education had provided me. Until then, however, my job was to gather the facts and then bring them to someone who knew what to do with them.

So, I recorded blood pressure results and noted chest pain complaints. I compiled CT scans, EKG results, and echocardiogram reports. I marked down symptoms and the nurses' observations, I took medical histories, and I studied each patient's chart.

I hunted and gathered data on my (actually, my attending's) patients, but I didn't know exactly what to do with it. I thought I did. For instance, I'd learned in medical school that an EKG checks for problems with the electrical activity of the heart. It's often ordered to find the source of unexplained chest pain, which could be the result of an impending heart attack but also angina or heart disease.

Taken by itself, the EKG may not identify a heart attack in the making. Or it may. More often, it's a piece of the medical puzzle, but we doctors never know how many pieces that puzzle has until we're well into the diagnostic phase, do we order tests, take histories, and gather data to help us finish that puzzle.

When I brought all the information to my chief fellow, he became impatient with me. "Well," he asked, "just how sick is the patient?"

I didn't have an answer.

What I didn't know then is that no matter how much information you gather, you can't make any decisions until you first figure out how sick the patient is. Without that data, you don't know where to start.

For doctors, meeting a patient is like dumping a box of puzzle pieces on the table. We have to start putting the edge pieces together so we have an outline for the work that needs to be done. "How sick is the patient?" is the equivalent of starting to put the edge puzzle pieces onto the table. Without it, terrible mistakes can happen.

Take, for instance the vascular surgeon who made the decision to "watch and wait" a patient with ischemic bowel disease, in which the arteries that supply blood to the intestines become narrowed or blocked. In its earliest stages, ischemic bowel disease is reversible, but in its later stages, surgery is required. This surgeon chose to wait for the results of an angiogram scheduled for the following week, yet forty-eight hours later, the patient's bowel failed and she died.

Ultimately, the surgeon made the tragic mistake of failing to determine how sick the patient was. He didn't set the correct starting point and failed to pick the correct ending point. See, much like putting down the edge pieces of a puzzle, every surgeon has to start with two points—one indicating where the patient is now, and one where the doctor thinks the patient is heading. Surgeons intuit how sick a patient is (point one) and estimate what the outcome might be (point two). Where we put the two points determines whether we're working slowly or quickly, in a straight line or in more of a rectangle, on a big puzzle or a little puzzle. And we're doing that all while knowing that we may need to move the points and therefore change our boundaries at any moment.

House Call

 This vacation, you're winging it. You're just piling into the car and heading up the East Coast, camping out along the way, or stopping at a motel or two. No need for reservations. No need to rush. But when you decide you want to visit Martha's Vineyard, you discover there's only one ferry ticket left for cars this week, a few hours from now. So you make the reservation and set your GPS for the fastest route to the ferry, getting there just in time. It's a matter of resetting your speed and your effort to fit the new situation.

Think of this part of the decision like it's a track meet with multiple events that all require different types of speed and strategies. Are we going to run the one hundred, giving it our all from the moment the starter gun goes off, or are we going to run the mile, pacing ourselves so we have some "kick" in the last half lap? Or is this not a race at all, but the high jump instead?

Whatever event it is, there's a starting point and an end point, and we need to know we may have to run the four hundred or the two mile instead. You never know.

In surgery, deciding at what pace to make decisions is as important as the decisions themselves. We never want to look back and think that we wasted time on an idea or a hunch that didn't pan out, or worse. And in surgery, it can be much worse. Determining how sick the patient is often turns out to be the most important decision we make, because it tells us where to start and aims us toward where to end.

How do we decide where the beginning is? Sometimes, it all starts with pointing to what hurts...which is the next rule in the Diagnose stage.

Gut Check

 When you approach a problem, take its vitals. Identify all the parts that aren't healthy, the areas that aren't working to full capacity and therefore need attention. Only then will you know how sick the patient is.

DIAGNOSE

Rule Two: Point to What Hurts

You can't start to diagnose the problem until you understand the core of the problem. Learning to boil the problem down to its chief complaint makes moving from the start toward the finish easier.

I can often tell just by looking at a patient that his appendix is about to blow, or that the bullet didn't hit any major organs, or that he's suffered a stroke. This part, the "What do we have here?" is rooted in intuition, and it's like starting with zero on the clock. Everything launches from this moment, so my initial question gets the diagnosis part clicking while I head into a phase of matching or refuting my own instincts.

From zero on the clock, I make my first move. I take a patient history and ask, "What brought you here today?" which is another way of finding out the patient's chief complaint. That complaint—stomach pain, nausea, or extreme fatigue, for instance—will help me make a list of possible diagnoses.

This part is exactly what we're taught in medical school, where we're told to gather information, such as the chief complaint, social and family histories, allergies, and so on. Sometimes, though, I just tell my patients to point. It's the fastest way to whittle down all the information to the specifics that I need to make a diagnosis.

See, sometimes when patients come in, they're so relieved to have a doctor hear them, they get mired in reporting too much. It's the "My knee hurts and my blood pressure was up this morning, and my brother was just diagnosed with cancer, so am I at risk?" Presenting too much information is totally understandable, especially when there's fear involved, but it can get in the way of weeding out the specifics. So what I do is ask the patient to point.

"With one finger, point to where it hurts the most," I instruct them, kids and adults alike.

Now I have something to work with. Now I have the most specific of the specifics: why the patient walked through the door in the first place. It's the very thing that made her stop and think, *I should see a doctor,* or *I need to go to the hospital.* Where she points helps me ask the right questions to reach the correct diagnosis. It's where we start the clock.

House Call

 You're on deadline, rushing to complete a project for a client, a department, or a higher-up. Suddenly, everyone involved in the project has an issue, something that he or she feels needs to be addressed right now or else you'll never get the job done. Instead of listening to the litany of issues (which you don't have time for), ask each one, "What's the real problem here?" That will help everyone boil down the problem to its core and clear out the clutter so you can fix the problem and finish the project on time.

If you've ever tried to soothe a hysterical kindergartener, you know how hard it can be to get to the root of the problem. There's sobbing, and tears, and stuff coming out of his nose. He's a bundle of raw emotions, and it's as though he's stuck in that state. If you tell him to calm down and stop crying, he cries even harder. If you ask him what's wrong, his sobs swallow his words, confusing things even more.

You give him a big hug to let him know you're there for him, and when he's a little calmer, you ask, "What happened?" Except now he's sobbing again, sobbing and pointing at the little boy who stole his toy truck. He's pointing at what hurts, or, more specifically, at what hurt him.

If he could get a hold of himself, he'd probably tell you the whole ugly story about how he was playing with his toy truck and another boy came out of nowhere and took it, about how he tried to get it back but the boy pushed him down while the other kids laughed, and then about how that boy took the truck to the other side of the playground, where he's been playing with it ever since, putting rocks in its flatbed and dumping them under the slide. All you really need to know is that some kid took his truck. When he pointed, you found that out.

Pointing works. As a surgeon, I use the answer to "What hurts the most?" to adjust my follow-up questions as I work toward a diagnosis. I ask a question relevant to where my patient pointed so I can start moving toward the end point. This means that I don't go down a list of predetermined questions in a particular order. The patient's answer determines the surgeon's next question, and the question needs to be relevant to that answer. What's more, I need to know when to stop asking questions and make a decision.

Let's say, for example, my twelve-year-old patient points at his lower right abdomen when I ask, "Where does it hurt the most?" Chances are, I'll think, *Appendicitis,* but if the patient suddenly feels better, I move appendicitis down my list of possible diagnoses and put gastroenteritis at the top, because appendicitis rarely improves on its own. I don't remove appendicitis from my list entirely, in case something else—a test, a symptom, a hunch—bounces it back up again. And I always keep the less common diagnoses, such as colon cancer, low on the list through this phase of adjusting.

While I'm adjusting my list of possible diagnoses, I'm sorting through them by asking the patient questions, taking his history, doing a physical exam, and so on. I'm checking what I'm feeling with my hands against what I'm feeling in my bones. If the patient's belly feels especially tender but he's barely registering the pain, I don't assume that my logic is wrong or that my gut made a mistake. I have to figure out why there's such an inconsistency before I move on to my next question.

This is because I've seen stoic farmers from Amish country present sicker than they'd let on, and I've had hysterical patients whose over-the-top emotional responses don't match the illnesses or injuries that I was about to address. Maybe the patient's belly is more tender than I'd expected, or maybe she's in shock and doesn't realize that she's bleeding from a bullet hole in her stomach. So I check their responses against my instincts, and then I gather more information. But I do this all before I start ordering tests, because if, for example, I let the stoic farmer's stiff upper lip guide my decision making, he could wind up dying inside a CT machine.

I ask a question, get an answer, check it against what I'm seeing and what I'm sensing, and then ask the appropriate next question. I adjust so I can narrow down the specifics as I head toward the diagnosis, all the while keeping in mind one of the most important axioms in medicine: The common things are common…the next rule of the Diagnose stage.

Gut Check

 This is the stage where you want to go from gray to black and white, from wide to narrow. You are winnowing down the problem to its core so you can make the correct decisions to address it. If you don't "point to what hurts," you just may misdiagnose the problem.

DIAGNOSE

Rule Three: Remember: Common Things Are Common
Common things are common because they happen far more often than the rare. When you're still in the beginning stages of determining what you need to do, rank the common above the rare, but prepare to change up the order as more information comes in.

The neurologist had already diagnosed the patient before he even asked her his first question. Based solely on the patient's chief complaint, which the nurse had jotted down, he was sure the patient had Wilson's disease, a rare disorder in which copper accumulates in the tissues, creating difficulties in walking, talking, and swallowing.

This, despite the fact that the patient had suffered a head injury in a car accident a year earlier. The doctor insisted that this particular piece of history was unrelated to her chief complaint, which was that her body's functioning had suddenly and dramatically worsened. She could barely walk, she was highly sensitive to light and sound, and she stuttered.

He started asking the patient questions to support his preselected diagnosis, dismissing answers that didn't fit his theory, and ordering (expensive and time-consuming) tests, which ultimately proved what the patient already knew: It *wasn't* Wilson's disease. Rather, it had very much to do with the brain trauma she'd suffered in the car accident. Not only did the neurologist fail to pay attention to what hurt the most, but he'd put rare at the top of his list without first considering that common things are common.

I see this a lot when a new study or paper about a rare disease comes out; suddenly, we have four or five new cases of this disease tentatively diagnosed at the hospital. It's a case of treating the rare as common—just like that neurologist did—and it can certainly be a blessing for the patient who actually has that rare disease. But chances are, it's nothing more than forcing a wrong diagnosis based on preconceived notions.

Now, wait a minute. Didn't I just say that surgeons start with an end point in mind? Yes, we do. But we also rank the list of possible diagnoses from most likely to least likely. Only after we review the patient's symptoms, history, chief complaint, physical exam, and test results do we start moving our diagnoses up and down our list. Only then do we adjust. That's not to say that the rare disease isn't on our list at all. It's just going to take more than a hunch (and costly tests) to move the rare diagnosis up above the most common ones.

For instance, in medical school, we're taught that right-sided abdominal pain generally nets a set list of diagnoses, including diverticulitis, appendicitis, Crohn's disease, viral gastroenteritis, enlarged lymph nodes (mostly in children), kidney stones, incarcerated hernias (Don't Google that!), bowel obstructions, urinary tract infections, and for women, ovarian abscesses or cysts, and ectopic pregnancies.

We list those like multiple-choice answers, knowing we have to *circle one.* Then we assign the patient's symptoms to the corresponding multiple-choice answers, adding symptoms such as nausea or moderate pain to the diagnoses that they fit, until one or more diagnoses appear to be most likely. It's like filling buckets in a video game; the bucket with the most symptoms will most likely be the "winner," *unless...*

The symptoms aren't the only factors we consider while we're adjusting our list. We also have to weigh patient history and test results. If, for instance, a twelve-year-old boy has a normal white blood cell count and a normal CT scan, but belly pain, I probably won't put appendicitis far down on my list, because chances are, we've caught him too early in the disease for the kind of test results we'd expect to get. But if an overweight forty-year-old man with no prior abdominal issues presents the same way, I may push appendicitis farther down on the list and start looking at kidney stones instead.

The process of putting the symptoms into buckets is what we call a "differential diagnosis," a systematic diagnostic method involving probabilities intersected with instincts. It's a cross between adjusting and remembering that the common are common. This is where science meets art, and I'm going to go out on a limb and say that art almost always beats science.

On paper, the boy with the abdominal pain but normal white cell counts and a clear CT doesn't have appendicitis. If his situation was a problem on a medical school exam, I wouldn't circle appendicitis as an answer, because, based on the science before me, he probably has something else. So, it's no wonder that residents fresh out of med school think this way, and it's no wonder that as chief of surgery, I'm constantly correcting residents' initial impressions. What they know is based on flow-chart thinking, whereas what we see in real life is rarely so black-and-white.

Remember, when you're evaluating, you're learning. The answers to our questions feed the diagnosis, and they also bring up new questions that can change the diagnosis. But we surgeons always have to have an answer—the *correct* answer. There's no "other" on our multiple-choice answers, which range, let's say, from A to F. One of them has to be circled. What we discover along the way could bump any one of them from B to F and then up to A. It all depends on what we learn during our evaluation, but chances are, the results will be something we see frequently, a diagnosis that's common.

House Call

 Your company spent a lot of money sending your boss to a big industry conference, so she feels like she'd better prove it was worth the investment. At her first meeting back in the office, she presents a hot new app she discovered on her trip that will automate the company's Facebook and Twitter posts. She proposes that it'll fix the lack of customer response your company has received on social media. She sets it up, and...nothing changes. Turns out the solution was far simpler: The posts never asked for feedback. Instead, they just broadcast company news, a common mistake among many businesses new to social media. If she'd looked for the common problems before treating the situation, she'd have found the right solution sooner.

When a plumber comes to your house to fix a problem, he'll bring in the tools he's most likely to use for the problems he most often sees. Plus, he'll make sure he has on hand what he needs for a sudden emergency, like water spewing everywhere, but he'll leave the special tool he uses once every few months on his truck because chances are, he won't need it. While he's diagnosing your plumbing problem, he's keeping the common problems at the top of his list: low water pressure, slow-draining sink/tub, running toilet, and stopped-up drain. He won't rule out the less common problems entirely until he's done diagnosing and has moved on to deciding.

Surgeons always put the imminently life-threatening diagnosis highest on the list. For example, if a patient comes into the emergency room complaining of chest pain and he's just eaten three breakfast burritos with extra hot salsa, the high probability is that he's suffering from gastric distress (high probability, but not certainty), so even though everything about the patient's presentation screams gastric distress, the physician must first rule out a potentially deadly heart attack. Or in the case of a boy with belly pain, we rule out appendicitis first.

Doctors are trained to look for horses when we hear hooves, so to speak. (As real doctors know, life is very rarely like an episode of *House*.) But we also have to keep in mind that there may actually be zebras. For every one hundred cases of appendicitis that I see, I may come across ten kidney stones, an ectopic pregnancy, and a food poisoning or two. If I don't keep my mind open while I try to home in on my diagnosis, I could miss something, so I'm always ready to adjust as needed. Ultimately, it's not *a* diagnosis that's vital but the *correct* diagnosis.

Finally, surgery, like many decision-based practices and businesses, is not archeology. Surgeons and their patients don't have the time to stop and examine everything along the way: every piece of patient history, every test result, every symptom. There are too many moving parts and too much at stake (and not enough time) to give everything equal weight and equal consideration. That's why the next important step is to keep in mind that not all information is created equal.

Gut Check

When you approach a problem, show up with your usual bucket of solutions first, keeping in mind that you may end up needing something less common to solve the problem.

DIAGNOSE

Rule Four: Reserve the Right to Change Your Mind

There's a difference between being wishy-washy and changing your mind. When you're faced with new and changing information, you need to be prepared to adjust your plan of attack as needed.

Your hands are inside your patient's body, and you're about to cut an organ. This is indeed a crucial moment, but not as crucial as every decision that went into choosing to make that cut. Are you sure that you've chosen wisely?

This is one of the reasons why the first few years of the surgical residency focus on diagnosis and patient management; we don't even get into the OR until year three. A surgeon needs all that experience in what happens before surgery in order to learn to make decisions that lead to (or away from) surgery. And one of those decisions may be to change your mind.

From the moment I meet a patient, I keep in mind that he could suddenly become sicker, which would move the end point I'd originally set rather quickly to the OR. Take, for instance, a ruptured spleen from a car accident. Most of these injuries will heal on their own without the patient being cut open, but there are situations in which emergency surgery is needed. If the patient is stable, I check the CT scan for fluid and wait. But if the patient isn't stable? The end point gets moved up, and we head into surgery immediately.

Surgery simply doesn't work on an "if-this, then-that" flow-chart system. Sure, there are surgical principles that do just that, but the whole picture from the beginning point of just how sick the patient is to the end point of discharge from care is far more complex than that. To make the right decision that helps the patient, surgeons have to be prepared to scrap their initial instincts and start over, moving more quickly or more slowly as needed along the way. This, before the first cut is even made.

House Call

 Think of those old movies in which a reporter with a breaking news scoop runs into the printing press room and shouts, "Stop the presses!" You have to be prepared to play that part if the information you receive changes your decision of what needs to be done. You need to stop everything and reevaluate.

Imagine you're an officer in the British Army arriving in Boston Harbor on April 18, 1775. Your army's plan is to march through the city and press westward to confiscate the Americans' arsenal along the route to Concord and capture patriot leaders Samuel Adams and John Hancock, who are believed to be hiding in nearby Lexington.

Except the Americans have other plans.

In fact, when the British arrive in the harbor that day, Paul Revere and William Dawes trigger an "alarm and muster" system that allows them to warn militia from Boston to Concord that the British are heading their way. (You remember: "The British are coming!") But when the British discover that the patriots are warning militia in neighboring towns, they stick to their plan anyhow.

Meanwhile, the Minutemen arm themselves and head west. After the Redcoats capture Revere and Dawes loses his horse, the Redcoats face down a band of Patriots on Lexington's common green. It is there that "the shot heard around the world" is fired, launching the American Revolution. By the time the British reach

Concord, they have fought and been defeated by five hundred militiamen, and they retreat all the way back to their ships in Charlestown in defeat, ambushed by armed Minutemen along the way.

Well now. That's not what the British had planned at all. If only they'd changed their minds and retreated earlier, they probably wouldn't have suffered so many losses, with the numbers of soldiers killed and wounded totaling around two hundred and seventy compared to the Americans' ninety, and the war might not have started, at least not that day. We might even be speaking in British accents and drinking tea today. But the British started out with one plan of attack and then failed to adjust quickly when the circumstances changed.

The need to adjust to outside forces happens in surgery, too. We start with how sick the patient is, which dictates how quickly to move—our plan of attack. Take, for instance, the recent case of an obese man with right-side belly pain. He was on steroids, which confounded our diagnosis because they were masking some of the pain. It was possible that he was sicker than he appeared to be. Radiology's report was vague, offering both ulcerative colitis and appendicitis as possible diagnoses, but only the latter would dictate a beeline to the OR. What should we do?

Something in my own gut told us to wait. That, plus the CT scan, the patient history, the side effects of the steroids, and the physical exam, prompted a decision: wait. Sure enough, twenty-four hours later, the patient's pain improved, ruling out appendicitis. We didn't get stuck on the first solution, which allowed us to change our minds even while we were in the middle of diagnosing the patient.

It has long seemed to me that this type of adaptable, changeable decision making belongs outside the OR—in fact, outside of medicine. Whether you're in business, sports, parenting, or any other area that requires efficient and quick decision making, the surgeon's shortcut to making good decisions can work, and work well. I know this, because I'm constantly testing it.

As a surgeon, I measure the results of my own decisions as I work. It's not as though surgeons collect data and then farm out the implementation of it. We don't make executive decisions that someone else tests, like an army general choosing whether his soldiers will storm the hill.

We surgeons *are* the people who carry out what we decide. We actually go inside the patient to solve the problem, which means that our decisions often come from the implementation of our prior decisions. We are the generals *and* the foot soldiers, so we not only make the decision to operate but also do the operation, and then we take the responsibility for what happens post-op.

We set the beginning and end points, and then we're there for the entire trip in between, no matter whether it goes in a straight line or a circle, quickly or slowly. And it all starts with those initial moments, checking in with our guts for a sense of where we are and where to go in the end. We take in how sick the patient is, how big or small or simple or complex the problem is. We take a snapshot of the situation, and we start the process. But first, we have to get to the specifics of the diagnosis, because not all information is created equal.

Gut Check

 Don't get married to the first solution you have. If you limit yourself to focusing on the same information and nothing else, you'll never discover what you need in order to change your mind and head toward the best solution.

DIAGNOSE

Rule Five: Not All Information Is Created Equal

Learning to give the right amount of significance to each piece of information in each case—as they relate to one another—helps you make better decisions.

The doctor sat at the edge of the cancer patient's bed. He had something important to tell her, but he wasn't sure where to start. The mother of two had been diagnosed with lymphoma, and soon, she would have to start four months of chemotherapy. He knew that one of the chemo drugs, toxic liquid derived from mustard gas, would likely render her sterile, and yet she was still of childbearing age. It was a difficult subject to broach, but as the oncologist who had diagnosed her cancer, it was his job to break the news to her.

"So, I need to tell you something you might not want to hear. … The chemo for lymphoma could make you infertile," he said. He was about to start his next sentence when the patient cut him off.

"Considering I had my uterus removed three years ago, this news is irrelevant."

D'oh! The doctor quickly flipped through patient's file, and sure enough, behind the CT report and the early pathology results, right there in the patient history, was the word: hysterectomy.

This missing piece of information turned out to be the most important one of them all, the one he should have looked at before he started his somber soliloquy, because it trumped everything else.

D'oh.

Even when you've got all the information in front of you—lab work, the physical exam, symptoms report, and patient history—

how do you know which one is the *least* reliable and which is the *most*? While it may be tempting to dismiss the information that you get from your patient as the most subjective and therefore the least reliable, that may not be the case at all. The simple truth is that *everything* must be taken with a grain of salt. There's no such thing as truly perfect information, even, for example, if it's coming from a multimillion-dollar CT machine.

On a CT scan, scar tissue can look like cancer, and appendicitis may not show up right away, so I have to check the results of all tests against the patient history, the chief complaint, the physical exam, and yes, my intuition. But it's not a painstaking process of spending the same amount of time and effort with each piece of information. Rather, I assign each piece of information its own weight depending on the variables of the situation. Only then do I start my own soliloquies.

House Call

 When you're buying a used car, how do you weight the information? The CARFAX® will tell you how many owners it's had, whether it's been in an accident, and what the service record says. The dealer will show you its new tires and Bluetooth hookup. Online reviews will share the model's average mileage (a plus) and its rough ride (a minus). It's up to you to weight them all against each other as they relate to your needs. Otherwise, if you let one fact (e.g., "It's so cool!") override the rest, you could wind up with a lemon.

In high school, homework, quizzes, tests, term papers, class participation, and exams are all weighted differently toward the total grade.

If a student spends the same amount of time and effort on a one-page worksheet as he does on studying for the final exam, he won't have any time for anything but that class.

A series of F's on his homework may mean that he doesn't understand the subject, or it may mean he's too lazy to do the homework. Those F's compared to his B on a term paper and an A– on the midterm might say more about the student's efforts in class (not to mention his understanding of weighting grades) than about his grasp of the subject.

It would be a mistake to look at the Fs and assume he's lost in math. If he's answering questions correctly in class and passing his exams, the teacher's "diagnosis" would be entirely different than if she'd assumed the Fs alone summed up the situation.

Likewise, in surgery, no one piece of information alone is greater in importance than everything else, and yet that's exactly how some doctors make a mistake in the Diagnosis part of the four D's: They give too much value to the one piece of information that supports their hunch so they can head toward that end point they'd set at the get-go.

For our colitis patient, we knew two things: Radiology couldn't rule out appendicitis, and the steroids he was taking could mask pain. Based on those things alone, we might have rushed him into a surgery he didn't need. Remembering that it's not just each piece of information that matters, but how each piece relates to the other, here, it's steroids mask pain *connected to* a noncommittal radiology report, *connected to* pain more on the flank than in the lower right belly, *connected to* a normal white blood cell count and no inflammation on CT, *connected to* a strong feeling that it isn't appendicitis. I took it all into consideration, yes, but I weighted each factor as it related to the others and also as it related to the top two diagnoses on my list (without completely ruling out anything else, just in case).

I take the long view so I don't get overwhelmed by the details, and I never hang my hat on any one test result, physical exam, symptom, or hunch. Meanwhile, I keep in mind this very important statistic: About 30 percent of abdominal pain goes undiagnosed. This doesn't mean, however, that a third of the time, I don't have to make a decision. Rather, my choice remains the same: surgery or no surgery. With no set diagnosis, it is, of course, the latter, but even then, I have to weigh all the information (though not equally) and head toward the second of the four D's: Decide.

Gut Check

 Resist the urge to override information that doesn't support your intuition. Assign it a weight and keep it in the mix, comparing it to other pieces of information until you're able to get to the point of making that diagnosis with confidence.

PRINCIPLE TWO:

DECIDE

The moment I reach for the door to the patient's hospital room to announce the diagnosis is the loneliest moment in medicine. This is when the decision on how to fix the problem rests solely on my shoulders. I've processed all the information, from patient history to lab results, run them by colleagues, checked them against my gut instincts, and have made a decision, a diagnosis. And that diagnosis had better be right, or else everything I do from here on in may not help—and could even *hurt*—the patient.

When you're a freshman surgeon, this moment is almost as daunting as the first time you're in charge of cutting open a patient. In some cases, it may be even more daunting, because at least when you're in the OR, you're surrounded by help. Remember, not only do we surgeons have to make a decision, it has to be the *correct* decision. Once we cut, it's cut, so everything we do hinges on the diagnosis: surgery or not, what to cut, how to cut it, and more.

No wonder it's easy to freeze here, to get stuck between these two D's: Diagnose and Decide. This is among the many reasons why surgical residencies are five years long. This time gives would-be doctors the experience of not only making the diagnosis but also of saying it out loud, of owning it. Life or death can lie in a surgeon's hands, a huge responsibility that should never be handed over to someone who hasn't been carefully educated, trained, and vetted. Ultimately, patients must be confident in their surgeons' abilities to make decisions and, more importantly, to make *correct* decisions.

Without a decision, nothing gets done, and that can be far worse than making the wrong decision. An infected appendix will continue to fester until it bursts. A perforated colon will keep spewing toxins into the abdominal cavity. Cardiac arteries will stay blocked, allowing vital heart muscle to die. Nothing is done unless and until a decision is made to do something. And as the surgeon, it's up to me to make that decision.

When a surgeon decides, it's kind of like the moment the referee hands the ball to the player for a foul shot. It's time to get ready for active engagement. You go from prepping for the shot to taking it, from determining the diagnosis to deciding on it. Go ahead: Lift the ball, take a breath, take the shot.

DECIDE

Rule One: There's No Diagnosis Until You Decide

Perhaps the hardest part of making good decisions is that moment when you have to stop gathering information and move forward. But without a decision, you'll never get anywhere.

You're just a resident. What do you know? Well, you're about to find out, at the mock orals, the training session for the real oral exams that you'll take to become a board-certified doctor…or not.

You enter the room where one of three (far more experienced and therefore intimidating) doctors offers you a surgical scenario:

"The patient, a fifty-year-old male, is throwing up blood. What's the first thing you do?"

You're nervous, no doubt about it. You don't want to make a mistake, especially under this kind of scrutiny. While you wrack your brain for your answer, the doctors prepare to determine three important things:

1. Do you understand the information?
2. Do you know what to do?
3. Are you a safe surgeon?

Trust me, after this, you'll never think the same way about making decisions, because in the board-certifying oral exams, experienced doctors—often those who literally wrote the books you've studied—will grill you to make sure that you can make good decisions on the fly. *Life and death* decisions. And you will either pass or fail.

So you're face-to-face with three seasoned doctors who have treated many real patients just like this fictional one. They know what to do, because they've done it over and over again. But you? You're new here. And you think that what you need now is more information. Your instincts are to ask the doctor a question, like "Is he a drinker?" or "Does he take an excess of acetaminophen each day?" but the doctor's question needs an answer, not another question, and your "patient" is throwing up blood.

"I send him to Radiology," you reply.

"The radiologist has left for the day," the doctor informs you. "Now what do you do?"

Um...

The ability to make a good decision is a learned skill, not an innate gift. Rather, it's conditioned and perfected with time and experience. As such, anyone can learn it, and anyone can get good at it, because at its core, it's an emotional process, not an intellectual one. The intellectual part comes in the Diagnose and Do parts. In Decide, however, you must have the ability to make your mind move forward, or else you never will get past Diagnose.

More than anything, deciding is an action, something you have to gear your mind up to do. It requires effort to process information into a solution and then share that answer. Like jumping the hurdles at a track meet, it requires an approach plus the purpose and energy to jump up and over the hurdle.

So, when it's your turn to make a decision, what do you do?

House Call

 If you've ever worked in a group, you've no doubt witnessed what happens when no one's in charge or when more than one person is in charge. The group gets mired in the information-gathering stage of the project, and then everyone sits around picking at the pastries and looking at their watches while no one makes a decision. The act of deciding requires focus and energy. Do you have it in you?

Consider the difference between browsing at the car dealer and choosing a car to buy. Window shopping requires a lower level of energy as you meander among the shiny new (or perhaps used) cars in a dealer's lot, reading the sticker prices and sipping coffee from a travel mug. This is the Diagnose phase, where you're collecting information and moving at a speed that matches your need for a new car.

But in Decide, you're down to one car, already having weighed the gas mileage, maintenance costs, practicalities, and price. You're picturing yourself driving the car with the windows rolled down and the radio blasting, and you're estimating the monthly payments. Meanwhile, there's a lot full of other cars behind you luring your attention.

This is go time, the time you make the Decision for one of the biggest purchases you'll secure, for the car you'll likely drive for years ahead. Are you sure this is the right one? Can you afford to buy it? Can you afford *not* to buy it?

If you don't make a decision, you may end up going home in your stinky minivan with 150,000 miles on it, wondering when that rattling noise will finally cause the engine to blow, leaving you stranded on the road with half the pee-wee baseball team inside. You need a new car, indeed. But is this the right one?

It's go time. It's time to decide. If you don't decide now, it's like you ran to the hurdle and stopped before jumping it. You need energy to get yourself over it. You have to push yourself to lift your leg and foist your body up and over. You have to decide, and you get to that point by calling it like you see it.

Gut Check

 Deciding on a diagnosis is a lot like lifting weights: You put yourself in the position to make a decision, and then you add energy to make it happen. Brace yourself, and then go!

DECIDE

Rule Two: Call It How You See It

Big decisions are still just decisions. When you let the size of the decision affect your ability to trust your gut, you'll freeze right when you're needed the most.

In surgery, the person who waits until all the pieces of information are in place is called a *coroner*. That's because the only time we can be absolutely certain of every single piece of information and what it means is when the puzzle is complete, which, unfortunately, is generally during an autopsy. Naturally, no one can afford to wait until then, least of all the patient!

This coroner logic is what trips up most doctors (and laypeople) while making decisions. The bigger the decision, the bigger the risk, and so we yearn for certainty. I've seen it with my residents who confess, "I know the answer, but I'm afraid to say it." What scares them is that once they share their decision, they've made the call. But that's exactly what they need to do.

When it's time to make a decision, it's like being an umpire or a referee: You've got to trust your eyes (and of course, your gut), and make the call—quickly and with confidence. Umps and refs know they've seen it hundreds or thousands of times: A strike's a strike, a foul's a foul, a goal's a goal. So they raise a hand with purpose, without doubt, signaling to everyone who's watching that they are confident in their decision. Don't let doubt creep in. Trust your eyes. Trust your gut. Go with your instincts and call it.

House Call

If you've ever been in a traffic jam, you know what it's like to finally reach the cause of the backup, only to discover that nothing's happening there. The accident has been cleared, and yet a line of traffic cones is still squeezing three lanes into one, while one cop sits in his car waiting for orders to move them. Sitting in that cop car is what it's like when you're afraid to call it how you see it. So go ahead and move it!

As a former college basketball player and an eternal sports fan, I see the real beauty of instant replay not in the one or two calls that are reversed but in the proof that the split-second judgments made by umpires and referees are almost always correct. They see it, and they don't hesitate to call it, because they know what they're looking at. After all, they've seen it before time and time again.

This is the virtue of trusting the gut at its purest, not to mention its quickest. The player's foot hits home base, and then the ball hits the mitt; call it safe. The defender's hand touches the ball right in front of the goal; call it a penalty kick. The wide receiver moves off the line of scrimmage before the snap; call it offsides.

The surgical residency teaches doctors-to-be how to recognize situations well enough to feel confident in their decisions and to reach a diagnosis—to call it, just like an ump or ref would. When you start to doubt yourself at the moment you have to call it, you create problems. But a strike's a strike, and appendicitis is appendicitis. I've seen it many, many times before, so I trust what I see (and the information I've already assessed), and I go with it.

But when I've declared my diagnosis—I've made my call—and I'm heading toward the OR when my appendicitis patient says she's suddenly feeling better, do I stop everything and reassess the diagnosis?

No.

Once a surgeon makes the decision to operate, he doesn't look back. Chances are, the patient started feeling better simply from the relief of having a confirmed diagnosis. How do I know that? Because I've seen it before! Besides, I trust my decision—my gut—because it's based on all of the principles of Diagnose that I went through to get to this point.

The patient's appendix will be removed, and then she'll never have to worry about it again. I've never left the OR without feeling better than I did going in. I call it how I see it, and that's the surgeon's way. More information, especially at that point, would only confuse things.

Gut Check

 You're not helping anyone by not making a decision. If it quacks like a duck, it is a duck. When you recognize what it is, call it. What's more, you need to call it with confidence, not cockiness (which, frankly, surgeons tend to lean toward). The difference is that confidence breeds success, as the saying goes. Cockiness, in contrast, reassures only yourself (and generally makes you look like a jackass).

DECIDE

Rule Three: Not All Decisions Are Created Equal

When you make decisions in a vacuum, you just might miss something very important. Always consider the scenario you're in before you apply any solution.

The patient seemed to be on the verge of a heart attack. The fifty-six-year-old male complained of sudden chest pain and shortness of breath, so the paramedic who had arrived at his home had placed him on oxygen. After making sure he had no allergies or contraindications, she had given him 325 milligrams of aspirin to chew. Then she had set about getting some important vital information, like his blood pressure, pulse, and blood saturation levels.

All the while, she kept talking to her patient.

"Is the oxygen making you feel any better? How's the discomfort now?"

Once she took her patient's vital statistics, she gave him a dose of nitroglycerin. His EKG results looked normal and he said he was feeling better, so she began to think that maybe he'd suffered instead from indigestion or anxiety.

Suddenly, the EKG monitor's alarm sounded. She knew what it meant: The patient was going into a life-threatening heart arrhythmia. She'd have to shock his heart back to a normal rhythm.

Based on the monitor, she would have been perfectly justified in zapping her patient with a tremendous jolt of electricity. There was just one problem: Her patient continued to talk to her calmly. In fact, when she asked him how he felt, he said that he felt much better after the nitroglycerin. His skin color and breathing had improved, and he denied any chest pain.

Though she prepared the pads in case she'd have to shock her patient, she didn't use them, choosing instead to monitor his progress by talking to him. Though the EKG monitor's alarm continued to sound, she made the decision not to shock the patient.

That, it turns out, was a brilliant decision, because a faulty electrode lead in the EKG machine—and not the patient's heart—had caused the alarm to sound. Her patient wasn't experiencing a life-threatening heart arrhythmia after all, and he remained stable throughout the ambulance ride to the hospital.

But what would have happened if the paramedic had decided to shock the patient based solely on what the monitor had told her? Very likely, she would have killed him.

Never make decisions in a vacuum, applying broad, textbook-style rules without taking into consideration the situation at hand. If you don't pay attention to what's happening right before your eyes, somebody just might get hurt.

House Call

 If you've ever taught little kids how to ski, you know that the basic rules sometimes need to be abandoned in a hurry. Say you've spent half the day on the bunny hill, teaching your charges to turn left and turn right and then snowplow to a stop, but when you get up on a steeper hill, one of them picks up too much speed and starts barreling toward a downed snow-boarder. She's forgotten how to turn, and there's no time for a textbook snowplow stop. There's only time for shouting at her, "Fall down now!" Now there's a good decision.

This part of Decide is a lot like investing. Too often, inexperienced investors get caught up in the moment and give too much weight to one piece of information, like financial news hype or a recent strong performance, but they don't take into consideration the situation they're in.

Say, for instance, you decide to go for potentially high returns from high-risk stocks because they've performed well since the 2008 crash. Look! They've gone up and up! And your coworker just made a bundle on XYC Corporation's stock, so it's gotta be a good investment, right?

So you plunk down your money on this one sexy stock, the same one that they're raving about on a finance show…and immediately lose a bunch of its value in a market correction. Now, if you were thirty-five and saving for retirement, that wouldn't be too big a deal, because you're in the market for the long run.

But you just gambled away a chunk of your seventeen-year-old's college fund because you didn't think about the situation at hand. You invested in a vacuum, and now you're paying for it. Literally.

The same thing can happen in the hospital when a surgeon decides that the best way to treat a patient with a bowel obstruction is by operating. Taken in isolation, that makes sense, but this particular patient also suffered major head trauma and spinal cord injuries in a car accident, and those must be addressed first. Operating on his bowel now might actually cause more long-term problems than it would help short-term ones—and we all know that doctors must first do no harm.

Sometimes, you make the right decision, but not for that scenario. That's why the decision you make in one situation may be different from the decision you would make in a similar yet not quite the same situation. When it's time to decide, make sure you "go wide" enough to see the whole picture, while being sure that you don't give too much weight to the wrong decision. And then you'll need answers, not more questions.

Gut Check

 When you're making a decision, take a moment to step back and look and the entire situation. How? Pretend you're presenting the situation to someone who intimidates you, someone who's also very impatient. You'll be amazed at how quickly you'll zoom out to see the big picture and reach the right decision.

DECIDE

Rule Four: No More Questions! Please!

When it's time to make a decision, it's time for an answer, not more questions. All too often, answering a question with a question only confuses the matter, leading you away from a decision instead of toward it.

It's my turn to be the intimidating, seasoned surgeon asking the questions in mock orals.

"The patient, a fifty-year-old male, is vomiting blood. What's the first thing you do?"

I don't want a question back; I want an answer. And yet, resident after resident still looks for that magical question, the one they think will provide the diagnosis and therefore the answers to the exam.

What they don't seem to realize is that surgeons treat the *patient*, not the *diagnosis*. For the vast majority of scenarios they'll ultimately encounter as surgeons (if they pass), they need one or two pieces of information to help treat the patient, like the one who's throwing up blood, or the one with the mass in his bowels. If the resident asks another question, he or she could wind up heading down a road that doesn't help the patient.

So, when I ask a question, I don't want a question back...and yet, this resident asks one. "Is he a drinker?"

The resident is trying to treat the diagnosis, but he needs that diagnosis first, and he's trying to get to it with the wrong questions. See, Radiology will reveal whether the patient has cirrhosis, a progressive destruction of the liver often caused by excessive use of alcohol. So the resident doesn't need that information at this moment to make a decision on how to treat the patient, because in 80 percent of diagnoses relating to vomiting blood, the initial treatment is the same, and I'm trying to find out if the resident knows what to do next.

"Give him fluids, install a Foley catheter, transfuse blood?"

I know what needs to be done, so I don't need a list of possibilities. I want to know what the resident would do if this patient were a real patient. As a result, an answer is the right answer. A question is not. Succeeding is about knowing when to stop asking questions and decide on an answer.

This scenario reminds me of that old TV show *Name That Tune* when a contestant would say, "I can name that tune in three notes," and her challenger would retort, "I can name it in two." No matter how few notes it took them to name that tune, they never needed the entire song. They know when they had enough to provide an answer.

Surgery is focused on problem solving, on doing something that improves the situation, which means that over the course of his training, the surgeon shifts his mentality from questioning to deciding. But too often in medicine, as in business, education, parenting, and any other situation in which you need to make a decision—especially a big one—people believe that asking more questions is an adequate substitution for an answer. That's a mistake. I know this, because I've seen its drastic results. Surgeons don't have the luxury of asking more questions, because while they're stalling, their patients could very well be dying.

House Call

 Have you ever gone to a restaurant with an undecider? You know the type: They pepper the waiter with incessant questions like "Does that come with coleslaw?" and "How is the tilapia prepared?" while your stomach starts to growl. Every question delays your dinner, and every answer prompts another question. Undeciders get lost in a tide of questions, while deciders fill themselves up. Although it may not matter much at dinner, it sure does matter at work and beyond.

If you've ever watched *Selling New York,* or any other real-estate TV show, you've no doubt seen what happens when buyers try to gather more information by seeing more apartments, as though more information will magically make an answer appear. And a big answer it is. These apartments go for millions, and yet they move fast in Manhattan, so the agent tries to explain that the apartment they're standing in matches the clients' criteria, such as location, number of bedrooms, nice views, and right price range, but the buyers hem and haw.

"We'd like to look at some other apartments," they say, while the agent sighs. She takes them to two, three, maybe even four or more apartments, but it turns out those aren't any better than the one the clients liked at the start, so they ask the agent to make an offer on that first apartment, only to find out that it's too late. While they were out asking questions about apartments that they didn't want, someone else bought the one they did.

Endless consideration makes the road to a good decision longer and more treacherous. You have to be able to recognize when you have enough information to make an informed, intelligent, and necessary decision—*and then make it.*

Gut Check

 Practice making decisions by giving answers instead of asking questions. When your conversations are weighed down by question after question, you will never reach your answer.

DECIDE

Rule Five: Stay on the Yellow Brick Road
When you treat a problem like it's more important than any other, it crowds out your time-tested and gut-checked diagnostic and decision-making skills. Stay the course, no matter what or who is involved.

Your patient has been shot in the chest. He has a punctured lung, and he's bleeding internally. Heavily. He lost three pints of blood on his way to the hospital, and he's in danger of going into shock.

This was no accident. The shooter wanted his victim dead. In fact, the .22 caliber bullet ripped through three inches of the victim's chest wall, ricocheted off a rib, sliced through the lower lobe of a lung, and came to a stop just one inch from his heart.

You insert a tube to relieve pressure from all that blood pouring from his damaged lung, and you get him ready for the OR.

Oh yeah, and the victim is the president of the United States.

This is exactly the scenario that surgeons at George Washington University Medical Center faced in March of 1981 when President Reagan, new to the office, was shot by John Hinckley Jr. And yet papers from the GWU libraries show that the presence of the biggest VIP in the country didn't change how the trauma team reacted or how the entire hospital functioned during his stay. Outside of the necessary increased security, the hospital made sure that there were minimal disruptions to other patients while the president recovered from the assassination attempt.

Dean of Medicine Dennis O'Leary called the operation "a relatively simple procedure." It took surgeons eighty minutes to stop the bleeding and remove the bullet, and President Reagan ultimately recovered completely, like many other gunshot victims before and after him. After all, his anatomy is no different from a drug dealer's, or a police officer's, or the sales clerk's from a held-up convenience store.

The surgeons did what all good surgeons do: They treated their VIP patient like any other. They didn't let emotion, stemming from the pressure of treating the leader of the free world, get in the way of their work. As a result, they didn't try overly hard to do their jobs.

What happens when you treat a patient (or a problem) like a VIP? You order another test that's probably not needed. You ask more people than usual for their opinions, which will likely cause confusion, not clarity. You consider options you wouldn't even think about under normal circumstances. Yet all that doesn't help the patient or solve the problem at hand.

House Call

 Why is it that whenever we do what we normally do, but do it for a VIP, we get flustered? Say you've made your famous chicken divan hundreds of times, and yet preparing it for your future in-laws makes you question every ingredient, the cooking time and temperature, and the presentation. Please, put down the salt shaker and get back to what you've done, and have done well, many times before! No sweat.

This situation, of course, reminds me of sports. Consider that you're a soccer player taking a penalty kick. Every single kick should be treated the same way: It's just the goalie vs. you, and you're trying to find the back of the net with the ball. Now imagine it's the final minutes of the World Cup championship game in a stadium with eighty thousand screaming fans and the pressure of your country pinning its hopes on you. Oh, and the score is tied. If you get the ball in the goal, your team—and your country—wins the biggest sporting event in the entire world.

But it's still a penalty kick. It's still the goalie vs. you. It's still about hitting the net behind the goalkeeper. Everything else is just a distraction, a narrative that doesn't change the fact that you have to run up to the ball, wind up your leg, and strike the ball with your foot. Whether you're taking shots at soccer practice or facing down your rival in the World Cup finals, you still have to go through the same process. Approach. Swipe. Kick. The circumstances will never change that.

Just like the ball doesn't care who's kicking it, in surgery, the pathology doesn't care who the patient is. A heart attack will kill you no matter who you are, and an appendix will burst no matter who it's in. A good surgeon (manager/employee/parent/teacher/administrator) learns to keep the surrounding circumstances from affecting the decision at hand.

Approach, swipe, kick.

Diagnose, decide, do. No matter who's watching.

Gut Check

 When it comes to solving a problem, concern yourself with what it is, not who it involves. How you manage the problem is always the same. How you manage the circumstances around it is an entirely different issue to address when you're not in the heat of making a decision.

PRINCIPLE THREE:

DO

All those years of learning where and how to cut is what separates us surgeons from other medical doctors. After all, we can't just prescribe a pill and wait to see what happens next. Much of the time, we have to open up our patients and manually fix the problem with our own hands. That's why so much of our time in medical school is spent on the act of surgery.

While our Diagnose and Decide stages may be similar to other doctors', our Do stage is decidedly different. What makes us good (or bad) surgeons is the sum of our performance in the OR. When we cut open a patient, it's game time, time to put everything we've learned, all we've decided, and all we can do out there.

It's no wonder surgeons are sometimes accused of having God complexes. Every doctor diagnoses and decides, but few do what we do. We put our hands inside our patients, cut out what's not needed, and fix what's "broken." We touch our patients' hearts—literally—and we come face-to-face with cancer. We hold our patients' lives in our hands, knowing that one mistake we make could render them worse...or dead.

It might then seem like the best way to do surgery is to go "slow and steady." Being methodical, working in a "daisy chain" fashion from one step to the next, would make sure that the outcome is positive, right? Slow down, take your time, and make sure you're covering your bases.

Well, in the operating room, slow and steady might actually put the patient in danger. The longer a patient is under anesthesia, the longer she's being subjected to the fundamental risks of surgery. As such, the sooner we can finish up the operation and move the patient into Recovery, the better off she'll be—assuming we've done our job well in the meantime.

In the OR, efficiency is king. Surgeons access a hundred years of surgical protocols and look for ways to improve their efficiency. We do that by focusing on what our hands are doing while simultaneously being aware of what needs to happen next and after that and after that, all the while staying alert in case something doesn't go according to our plans.

Those plans are the key to successful surgeries. The act of surgery is a good deal more than taking the patient into the operating room and starting to cut. While we employ a specific, tested, and proven surgical process for every single surgery we perform, we also keep in mind that the whole thing could go to hell in a handbasket at any moment.

Though we no longer perform surgeries in operating theaters before an audience of onlookers, the operating room is, in fact, like a stage for us. We've memorized, rehearsed, and prepared, and now it's show time. We follow the script, yet ad lib where needed. It's time for the performance, to do what we do best.

DO

Rule One: Any Idiot Can Do One Thing at a Time

Multitasking helps you get more done in a day, but only if you do it right. If you overlap your techniques, you start new tasks while leaving room to finish old ones.

My own father told me that I'm too dumb to be anything but a surgeon. As an interventional cardiologist who installs heart catheters and artery stents into his patients, he claims it doesn't take a genius to take something out.

Very funny, Dad.

Among doctors, surgeons are sometimes seen as the dimmest bulbs in the hospital, because the core of what we do is mechanical. We follow set procedures of modern surgical principles that pretty much have been around for the past hundred years. Except for in robotic surgery, laser surgery, and endoscopy, today's surgeons are essentially cutting the same way the grandfathers of modern surgery did.

I like to think it's because we make what we do look easy. It might seem like we're just doing one thing at a time, but really, we're doing one thing and thinking about many other things—but the *right* things. We're watching the big picture, yet managing the details at the same time. Basically, we're multitasking in what I call timesharing, a system that eliminates waste by combining steps or freeing up time during one task to start another.

Picture a series of Venn diagrams, in which two circles overlap. In that overlapping area is where procedures and tasks from one surgery or project also fall into the procedures and tasks from the next one. Being efficient means putting as much in that shared area as you can. This way, more tasks are accomplished at the same time. If we didn't do that, the four or five surgeries that a surgeon typically performs in a day would take upward of eighteen hours.

Now, that would be dumb.

When I'm heading to the hospital for rounds, I call my chief resident to get the work started. We compare notes on patients, enter orders for meds, tests, and procedures, and plan ahead. Then when I get to the hospital, our rounds take just ten minutes instead of twenty. Later, I use downtime after a colonoscopy to schedule another one, time-sharing each procedure with my office hours. If I overlap in six different areas (six sets of Venn diagrams, side by side), I can get out of work an hour earlier and go hit golf balls.

I am not alone in relying on this technique. I once watched a heart surgeon at the Cleveland Clinic manage multiple bypass surgeries in one day by overlapping tasks the same way. This allowed him to efficiently fit more surgeries into an eight-hour workday than other surgeons usually do. He started his first surgery of the day in one operating room, and about an hour later, his assistant made the initial incision in a second patient in the next operating room. An hour after that, a third patient's surgery would begin.

As soon as the surgeon finished the vital part of the surgery—the actual sewing in of the bypass—in the first operating room, he headed over to the next room to begin the next bypass. As he took over sewing in that bypass, his assistant went to the first room to finish the operation on the first patient.

And so the process went throughout the day. Each patient had the benefit of one of the best heart surgeons performing his or her bypass, because time-sharing allowed him to do each surgery, all with enough time to follow up on his patients in post-op and make sure they were progressing well.

House Call

 When you're driving, you can't concentrate just on the road right in front of you. You have to be aware that the car in front of the car ahead of you just slammed on the brakes, or that a deer just appeared on the side of the road a few yards ahead. Work like you drive (or should drive), and you'll be able to incorporate what you're doing now with what you need to plan for in the near future.

This rule is kind of like those Food Network TV shows where the chefs compete to cook fast and cook well, only surgery is generally less harried: The chef gets the roux reducing in one pan and then pops over to the oven to baste the chicken. Then she chops the green onions while shouting to her partner to roll out the dough for dessert. Surely she is paying close attention to the knife she's wielding, but at the same time, she's planning ahead. It's an extreme version of the time-sharing technique, and without it, the show would run out of time long before the chef got everything ready for the tasting.

She's taking advantage of the gaps in the process, such as waiting for water to boil or the roast to finish cooking, and filling them in with things on her to-do list. She's planning ahead one, two, three steps or more, and finishing it all efficiently by time-sharing what she can. This sort of overlapping takes advantage of the "dead space" during tasks, allowing you to accomplish more in less time, whether you're cooking dinner or cutting open someone's abdomen.

Keep in mind that surgeons who time-share are "looking for assassins." We keep asking ourselves, "Who's trying to kill my patient now?" While we're operating, we're thinking ahead: "Is the nurse going to hand me the wrong instrument?" or "Did Anesthesia forget to tell us the patient had low blood pressure?" or "Is my resident about to perform the wrong stitch?"

The more efficient I am at time-sharing, the more efficient the entire surgery becomes…which is why it drives me absolutely bananas when one of my nurses effectively works against my time-sharing technique. Take the nurse who forgot to have on hand the stapler—the one that helps me close up a patient's belly. She had to go out of the room, down the hallway, into another OR, and into the drawers to find one. Meanwhile, I was standing there with my hands inside the patient, waiting to close, and thinking about my next surgery.

Time-sharing may seem like a little thing, but in surgery, it's not. It's wasting valuable time that has a ripple effect on all the surgeries in that OR and on my docket for the day. If the nurse had planned ahead, we wouldn't have missed a beat, and the surgery would have been over by then. Plan, time-share, and do.

Now, that's smart.

Gut Check

 Combine tasks that use similar tools or processes so you can save time. The more time you shave off your plan, the more efficient you'll be. But resist the urge to start too many things at once without finishing any of them. That's not time-sharing; that's creating a mess and complications.

DO

Rule Two: If You Don't Know Where You're Going, Any Road Will Get You There

Once you decide on a diagnosis, all that's left is carrying out the plan, yet the plan is where some of the biggest mistakes are often made. If you create a map by starting at the end and working backward, you'll be able to avoid complications that can send you off course.

My patient needed to have twelve inches of his colon removed. That was the end game, the decision based on the diagnosis: a septic infection in his bowels that caused fever, bloating, and abdominal pain. Worse, his life was in danger, as toxins were leaking out of his colon and into his abdomen. He'd been struggling at home for days when he finally came to the ER in severe pain. We determined that he'd suffered from perforated diverticulitis, a hole in his colon. It was up to me to fix it. I'd open him up, cut out the infected section of his bowels, and resect, or sew back together, the healthy parts.

I knew where we were headed, but I also knew what could go wrong along the way. On the left side of his colon, I'd have to steer clear of his ureter, which carries urine from the kidneys to the bladder. On the right, I'd have to be careful not to accidentally slice open his duodenum, the part of the small intestine that connects to the stomach. Plus, I'd have to be mindful of the blood vessels and arteries throughout the area to avoid causing any unnecessary bleeding.

I couldn't just cut him open to have a look-see and then figure out where to go. Surgeons don't tinker. I told my resident we had a plan based on the end result: removing a foot of his colon and avoiding the potentially dangerous spots while cutting where it's both safe and effective. We'd know ahead of time that the ureter likes to crimp up at a particular point, so we'd have to dissect it in a different spot. After we sewed together the remaining healthy parts, we'd close, put the patient on antibiotics, and see how he did.

The patient did fine. After a few days, he showed no signs of complications, fever, or pain (outside the expected post-surgical kind), so we sent him home.

Here in the Do part of the process, our chances of making mistakes that lead to complications increase, so we surgeons go in with a plan, working backward from our goal. Only when we know that we have to remove the infected portion of a colon do we know where to cut first—and what to avoid cutting.

House Call

 Planning backward works outside the OR, too. Say you're preparing a speech you'll present to five hundred people. Don't start with your opening remarks, the "Thank you to the association for inviting me to speak." Rather, start with the ending. How do you want your audience to feel? What do you want them to take away from what you've said? Then work backward, outlining the main points and avoiding the traps that could send you on tangents.

Think of this rule like golf, which I love to play. I see where the hole is, hundreds of yards away. That's the end of my plan. There are sand traps on the left and far down on the right that I have to avoid. If I slice my ball to the left, I'll wind up in the woods. If I hit to the right, my ball will land in a pond. So I plan from the end backward, figuring out where I'll need to aim my tee-off in order to hopscotch my way to the hole. If I end up hitting my ball into the trees, I change my plan, but the end point remains the same: get the ball in that hole.

When we know where we're going, in golf as in surgery (as in life), we can plan ahead—far ahead. We think not just of the first cut or shot or step but also of the ones after that as well. Surgeons don't just show up beside the patient and make an incision without first imagining the end result. Sure, every surgery has three to five clearly delineated steps unique to each type of operation, but only when we think far ahead can we evaluate what we'll need to do between those steps.

What's more, thinking far ahead allows us to imagine beyond the surgery to the possible complications to the patient's quality of life. Sometimes we even have to perform a series of surgeries, as in the case of my patient who'd had a serious motorcycle accident. The first surgery relieved pressure on his brain, whereas the second involved fixing a femur fracture with a pin in his leg. The third and final surgery repaired his damaged spleen. Every surgeon involved in caring for this patient plotted out the subsequent surgeries and the end game of a cure for his injuries.

We had a plan, and we followed it, steering clear of the sand traps and water hazards, and reevaluating each step as needed. By starting at the end point and moving backward, the surgeon is able to evaluate the more difficult parts of the process. The same is true for any plan you've made from your own diagnoses and decisions: You just have to remember to start at the end.

Gut Check

 The Do stage is where some of the biggest mistakes can happen, because you're focused on what's in front of you, not on where you're headed. You can avoid complications by planning backward, like you might with a maze. That way, you can see where you need to go once you get to the start, and you can plan accordingly.

DO

Rule Three: Know Where the Exits Are

When you get to the action part of your plan, know how to get out in case there's trouble.

You're in the middle of a routine colon resection when suddenly, your patient's blood pressure drops dramatically. He's having a heart attack. You have to get him out of your OR and over to ICU, but his bowels are still cut open. Worse, his colon might leak toxins into his abdomen.

What do you do?

You put in a drain, temporize the area, and divert fluids from his colon into a bag outside his body, thereby preventing infection. It's basic plumbing, performed in a big hurry. Then you send him off to the ICU to save his life.

This is an example of the old fight, flight, or freeze reaction to a sudden dramatic change, but in the middle of a surgery, flight and freeze aren't options. You can't just quit and go home, leaving the patient unconscious and sliced open! If we freeze, our patient just might bleed out, so we fight. It's our only choice.

Oh, and this scenario didn't really happen (though it likely has many times over in hospitals around the world). Rather, it's a classic question from the board exams, designed to test doctors in training to see if they know where the exits are.

Before we even start a surgery, we have to know how to get out of trouble fast. There's no time to figure out the process when chaos strikes, so we study possible scenarios, and determine how to fix them, and fix them fast, when the patient is fictional. Then if the real thing happens, we're ready to close up and get out as quickly as possible.

You know how you tune out the flight attendant when she's telling you where the emergency exits are? You're all comfy in your seat and looking forward to diving into the magazines you bought in the terminal, and she's all, "Blah, blah, blah," about what you should do if something goes wrong.

Okay, so maybe you've heard what she has to say a bazillion times, and this time seems no different, but she's telling you how to get out of the plane in case things suddenly become uncomfortable while you're up in the air, perhaps over a large body of water. Learning how to use your seat as a flotation device and noting where the nearest exits are will sink into your head better without the chaos of screaming people, crying children, and catapulted magazines around you.

So, prepare for trouble before it hits, even—and perhaps especially—if that trouble is something you've caused.

There's an old joke that comes from the OR that fits here:

> Nurse: I heard your surgeon say a four-letter word during the operation.
>
> Patient: Oh no. What did he say?
>
> Nurse: "Oops!"

Naturally, we plan for the oops and the complications. We go into surgery with a plan in mind, but we're always ready to adjust that plan efficiently and effectively the moment something goes awry, and to head for the exits.

Sometimes, however, the answer is just a matter of moving elsewhere for a while. In fact, we have a saying in surgery: "When the going gets tough, go somewhere else." Take, for instance, my patient with a stubborn tumor, which had adhered to her colon like a piece of dried cement, making it hard to remove.

I started in an area that seemed easy to dissect and began chipping away at the cancer. Soon, though, I realized that I wasn't getting anywhere, so I tried a different angle. Then I cut from the left, then the right and then the bottom. Chip. Chip. Chip. Whenever I got too deep into the colon wall, I chipped away at a different part of the tumor. Whenever I got too close to a blood vessel, causing the patient to bleed a little, I moved somewhere else, and then back to the beginning, where, suddenly, it was easier to work.

If I'd blindly plowed ahead with my surgical plan, I'd likely have caused damage by forcing the tumor out. I could tear healthy tissue from the colon wall or poke a hole in the patient's bowel, or I could rip open a major blood vessel and cause excessive internal bleeding. So, whenever we surgeons run into a difficulty, rather than toughen up and barrel forward, we can simply shift to another point of attack, one that maintains the safety and well-being of our patient. The principle here is to always move from unsafe toward safe, and whenever our movement becomes too unsafe again, we shift and find another safe place to go forward.

What's more, when we operate, we want to see ahead of the dissection, constantly thinking about what might happen one or two steps ahead of where we are. We never want to "cut blind," which puts our patients at risk for complications that diminish the efficiency of the surgery. It's always smarter and more efficient to work in an easy place than in a difficult one. The trick is finding the easier spot to work, so we keep chipping and moving, chipping and moving, until we complete the job in the safest way possible.

I thought of this surgical rule while watching my friend's son play with his new remote-controlled toy truck. Though he loved to play with it, he wasn't particularly good at driving it. Rather than steering his toy truck through the open doorway, he often hit the wall with it. Instead of backing the truck up and turning to avoid the obstacle, he'd just bounce it off the wall again…and then again…and again…and again. No matter how many times he'd hit the wall, nothing changed (except the addition of more and more marks on the wall, perhaps). He was moving forward, but really, he wasn't, because he didn't bother to try to find an easier way to go.

So, how do you prepare yourself for those tough times? By recognizing what could go wrong, creating alternate plans ahead of time, staying cool when the proverbial fan gets hit, choosing fight over freeze or flight, and finding a different way in (or, if needed, out). In other words, if you can't chip here, chip there and then come back later. When the going gets tough, the tough go somewhere else. If necessary, they simply head for the exits.

Gut Check

 Whenever you hit a barrier to fixing your problem, think of a piece of gum stuck to your best piece of furniture. If you yank it off, you'll rip off the finishing with it, so you chip at it from different angles until it finally gives—without a piece of your coffee table stuck to it.

DO

Rule Four: Know the Speed Limit

Different parts of your plan require different speeds. The answer isn't to work like the Tortoise or the Hare. It's the Tortoise and the Hare, taking turns as the project warrants.

You're so close to going home when, darn it! You've been called in for a clogged artery at the end of your shift. Normally, this procedure can take upward of two hours to perform, but not for you. Not today. You've installed so many stents before, you could do this in your sleep. You scrub in and make the incision for the catheter, no problem, quickly and easily. You zoom on over to the arteries surrounding the heart and prepare to install the stent, a small metal mesh tube that works like scaffolding for the blocked artery.

And then you slow the heck down.

You insert the balloon into the cylindrical stent to open it up, effectively giving the patient a momentary heart attack as you cut off the blood flow to his heart to install the stent. This part, you never rush, because it's the most arduous point in the procedure, the point where complications are most likely to arise. Like when you slow down for a patch of ice on the road, you're more deliberate and more alert, no matter how much you want to get home right now.

Different parts of each surgery proceed at different speeds. Generally, we surgeons open and close quickly. In fact, many incisions are now closed with staples rather than stitches, making the process even more efficient. And fast.

In between opening and closing, however, we adjust the speed to the task at hand. For instance, we might joke around on our way into a colon resection, but once we're inside, it's a different story. When it's time to fire the stapler that connects the two healthy parts of the colon, we slow down considerably to give this our most heedful attention. This is not a quickie stapling job, a close-and-go. It's a tricky procedure, in which the surgeon has to insert a stapler, which looks nothing like the one on your desk, into the two resected ends of the bowel, employ a circular scalpel within the stapler to cut away excessive bowel, and then staple together the two healthy parts of the bowel with a twisting motion.

If you were watching the surgery, you'd sense that we'd begun to move more slowly and deliberately the moment our open was done. The tone of the room changes as the speed adjusts to each part of the surgery, especially one this complex. Everyone at the table slows down in concert until it's time to speed up again. We know how fast, and how slow, to go.

House Call

 There's always at least one person in the office who consistently works at the same speed: slow. Your emergency doesn't make her move any faster, and so sometimes you have to find a way to work around her to keep the project going. Similarly, there's always the one person who's busy-busy-busy and wants you to keep up. To her, everything is a crisis and everything has to be done right now. They're both right, at least part of the time, but the key to working smart is to know when to speed up and when to slow down, no matter what's going on around you.

This rule, of course, reminds me of driving, specifically in Manhattan. A friend of mine who had moved to New York City from Los Angeles was taken by the way the traffic moved together from stop light to stop light in the Big Apple, speeding up and slowing down almost as a unit. If a double-parked car blocked the left lane, a car would slow down to avoid it, and the taxi just behind him in the next lane would slow down, too, to let him pull ahead. Now in the same lane, both the car and the cab would speed up with the rest of the traffic. Sure, there's always one jackass who thinks he owns the road, but the rest of the traffic quickly spots him and adjusts to his out-of-sync movement.

The funny thing about it, my friend said, was that he'd never seen anything like that in LA. "If a car slows down in a lane in LA, someone's going to crash, because drivers there feel possessive about 'their' lanes," he observed.

Now, I'm from Pennsylvania, and so I can't really comment on LA drivers, but I have been to New York City, and so I know what he means. The way New York drivers move in sync is a great metaphor for surgery, where you need to know how fast to go, and also how slow, to keep the whole operation moving smoothly. Move too fast, and you could get into trouble. Move too slow, and not only won't you get there in time, you'll hold up everyone else. When it comes time to get moving, know your speed limits, and go your speed limits.

Gut Check

 Going one speed, like in a stock car race or on a lazy-river water ride, doesn't take into consideration how each part of your plan needs to be treated. Be prepared to speed up or slow down as you finish what you've planned. If you're going one speed the whole time, you're doing something wrong.

DO

Rule Five: Beware the Easy Cases

If it seems too easy, it probably is. Resist the urge to coast through projects that appear to be no-brainers. It's often the seemingly easy cases that cause the most trouble.

It was an easy cardiac case: fifty-year-old male, one blockage, one bypass. I figured that the attending on my heart surgery rotation would be relaxed. I mean, this was a straightforward surgery, nothing fancy—certainly nothing as harrowing as the re-operations we'd done on frail eighty-year-olds. Our patient was relatively young and otherwise healthy, so the procedure was pretty much a textbook case for a cardiac surgeon, straightforward and uncomplicated…and yet, the surgeon had complications on his mind.

"This is the one when nothing bad can happen," my attending warned me about the easiest operation we'd had all week. He knew we had to beware the easy cases.

My sister the malpractice attorney can tell you that the easiest cases are often the ones that go awry. It's during the routine appendectomy, the one among thousands of more complicated surgeries, when you slip up, mostly because you're not as focused as you are during the tough jobs. When it looks easy, you're tempted to move too fast and pay less attention. And then you're the one saying, "Oops."

In fact, one of the most common malpractice suits happens after a young and otherwise healthy person has surgery to remove gallstones and the gallbladder. It's a routine surgery with little risk for complications. Pretty much all a surgeon has to do is snip the duct that connects the gallbladder to the body, sew it shut, and take out the organ.

So a seasoned surgeon who's done hundreds of these surgeries might take it less seriously, perhaps yapping with the nurse about what to get for lunch while cutting open the patient. He'll clamp, snip, and...uh oh! Instead of cutting the gallbladder duct, he's just snipped the liver duct.

Now instead of having an easy surgery to do, he's got a time-consuming and complicated operation that includes reconstruction of the liver duct. He probably also has a lawsuit brewing, all because he didn't beware the easy case. Any time it feels easy, take it as a warning to be more careful. Otherwise, you just might do all the wrong things. Here's where you tend to skip right through the principles you understand, because you figure that nothing can go wrong with something so uncomplicated: ,

- **You do one thing at a time.** You fail to think ahead a few steps, leaving you to stand there and wait to close while the nurse goes down the hall to find the surgical stapler.

- **You don't know where the exits are.** You don't plan for complications, because you don't think any can happen during such a simple operation.

- **You don't go somewhere else.** You barrel through with your surgical plan, causing unnecessary complications like bleeding or tears.

- **You don't follow the speed limit.** You speed up and stay sped up, even when you should really slow down and pay closer attention.

As a result, the hardest lessons often come from the easiest cases.

House Call

 On paper, you're a shoo-in for the job. Compared to the other applicants, you have more experience, and you're the best match for the skills they're looking for, so instead of prepping, you slack off. You sleep a little later, skip reading over your resume, and stop for coffee on the way to the interview. Not until you're in the waiting area do you spot the glaring typo on your resume and the fact that your socks don't match each other. Then you spill coffee on your jacket. All because you treated the interview like it was easy.

Consider your easiest high school class. Let's say you are a math whiz who barely studies and still gets A's in algebra, so the night before a run-of-the-mill test, you glance over your notes and then figure you'll wing it.

The next day in class, the teacher places the test on your desk and you start rushing through the questions.

These are easy, you think as you slap down X's here and multiply what's inside the parentheses there. You finish ten minutes ahead of everyone else and spend the rest of the time reading *Huckleberry Finn* for English class.

But when you get the test back the next day, you discover that you got four of the ten problems wrong. It seems that you mistook all the negatives for positives, and vice versa, setting you off on a trail of errors that left you with a big fat D on what should have been the easiest test of the semester.

Oops.

That's why in surgery, when things seem to be going easy, we slow down and stay alert to avoid dumb mistakes. Zipping through the easy cases is a sure way to invite Murphy's Law to set in, causing complications, and, quite possibly, lawsuits. Just ask my sister.

Gut Check

 Anytime you have the urge to treat the task at hand like it's simple, think "upset." How many sports teams at the top of their brackets have gone into games against the bottom-ranked teams all cocky and complacent, only to have their butts kicked in what should have been the easiest game of the season? Now, that's upsetting.

DO

Rule Six: One and Done: Do It Right the First Time

Avoid having to ask for do-overs. They're often embarrassing and confusing, as you try to both complete the job and clean up your mess. Learn to get it right the first time, and your work will go more smoothly.

Your insides aren't meant to be touched, let alone cut. That's why they're on the inside! Nobody learns that faster than a surgical resident who's attempting to suture injured tissue for the first time. Stitching a resected colon is like trying to sew together pieces of wet tissue paper. It's easy to foul up, for instance, by creating a five-millimeter hole where a two-millimeter one was. Now you've got a patch job instead of a stitch. It's more work, *messy* work, and it not only takes longer but also invites complications.

Your body simply doesn't like to be manipulated on the inside, so every stitch and every touch changes the quality of the tissue. In short, the tissue gets cranky, so when you take six stitches to do what should be finished with five, you risk injuring the tissue even more, perhaps even tearing it. As a result, we surgeons have a mantra: "One and done." By doing it correctly and precisely the first time, you minimize to almost zero the possibility of having to go back and do it again, this time on cranky tissue.

See, efficiency lies in the sweet spot between time and energy savings and a successful outcome. It's not a fixed spot; it's constantly changing from patient to patient and procedure to procedure. And its enemy is the foolish shortcut.

House Call

 In construction, there's a saying that also fits elsewhere: "Measure twice, cut once." In other words, get it right the first time, because if you don't, you'll have more work to do to make up for your mistake before you can finally get the job done. You can minimize errors by avoiding unproven shortcuts and cutting the right thing at the right time.

A friend of mine recently set out to have her deck repainted in time for her daughter's engagement party. Ever on the lookout for a bargain, she hired the least expensive painter she could find, someone who, I suspect, was really a home improvement guy who didn't do a lot of painting. She also chose the cheapest paint that would "do the trick."

Her painter actually did a great job. It's a good thing, too, because he had to paint her deck twice (and was therefore paid twice)—once with the cheap paint and then with the good stuff that she had to buy when the cheap paint looked awful on her deck. In the end, she wound up paying as much money as she would have if she'd hired a professional painter, someone who likely could have warned her not to use the cheap paint in the first place.

It's important to realize that "one and done" can be possible only if you tap into other people's expertise. In surgery and in life, we are fortunate not to have to reinvent the proverbial wheel every time we do something. I learn directly from the experiences of other surgeons past and present. Every mistake they made and every insight they amassed become part of my knowledge base. Their experience informs my own, and I'd be foolish not to tap into it while I've got my patients' organs in my hands.

When a procedure calls for five stitches, it doesn't call for four or six. The reason we know that five is the correct number of stitches in the procedure is that the common experience among generations of surgeons before us has proven that five stitches brings about the best results.

The first step in doing something just once and doing it right, a one and done, is to be precise. When surgeons get into trouble, it's usually because they muck around, trying to fix something that isn't broken. They complete one step and then stop to view it from all sorts of different angles to be sure it's "okay," but if they'd followed the tried-and-true rules of precision while simultaneously trusting their guts from the start, they'd have a better chance of getting it right the first time.

Gut Check

 Sir Isaac Newton wrote, "If I have seen further, it is by standing on the shoulders of giants." In other words, rely on the expertise of those who have done it before, and you, too, will be able to get it done and done well. This goes not just for careers that have been around for a long time but also for the newer ones.

DO

Rule Seven: Build a Body of Skills

When you build a body of work instead of treating each project and each job as a situation you've never experienced before, you avoid wasting time and energy.

Every single surgery that a plastic surgeon I know does is a difficult one—or at least she makes it look that way. She sets up her OR with every suture and every surgical doodad you can imagine, as though she's preparing for the most complicated plastic surgery known to man (or woman). As a result, even the simplest procedures can take her upward of seven hours, when other equally capable surgeons can do the job in two. She makes a difficult case out of the easiest ones, and it's eating up her time and energy.

My father has no patience for people who like that, doctors who "muck around." This from a man who can do twenty heart catheter installations in six or seven hours—and do them very well—while other cardiologists generally complete half that number in the same amount of time. He manages this by treating the core of his cases like a body of work rather than as thousands of individual situations.

What I mean by that is that he's learned to streamline the repetitive parts of his work, which in turn makes what he's working on more predictable. This predictability then allows nurses and surgical assistants to better anticipate his next step, which adds to the efficiency of the surgery. When you "keep it simple, stupid (surgeon)," you make whatever you do easier to repeat.

Naturally, when you're starting out in surgery, all of your work will feel grueling, so each case will land in the eight-to-ten range of the scale of difficulty, but with experience, the appendectomy that once took you an hour will take ten minutes, moving it down into the one-to-three range. Your body of work then begins to spread out on the scale so you have clusters, from the easiest to the most difficult, with many falling in between. Then you won't need every suture in the OR with you every time.

Like my father, I want the experience of one hundred cases, not one hundred experiences of cases. Following the same steps for each procedure means minimizing mistakes. How? When you systemize your work, you streamline the process, which increases efficiency. The scalpel is always in the same location, and the equipment I need is never in the room down the hall, so the scrub nurse is always ready with both. The first assistant focuses solely on her jobs of suturing, controlling bleeding, and handling tissue. The chief resident handles the close.

This stage is about eliminating clutter so you can get the job done. I don't have to stop to examine every part of every situation, because I've seen it all before, over and over again. It's like I keep all that information and all my experience in one doctor's bag in my head. That way, I always have what I need at hand.

House Call

 Let's say you're a writer with a 250-word blog post to write. Easy, right? You can't give it the same intense effort that a 250-page book requires. That's not to say that you slap down just any old thing for the blog, though. You're a professional no matter what you're working on, but the short blog post lies at one on the difficulty spectrum, while the labor-intensive and lengthy book falls at ten. Any time you write, you you draw on your experience with other blog posts and other books to systemize what you need to do in an effort to streamline the process, no matter what you're working on.

When it comes to building a body of skills, think *Groundhog Day* instead of *Fifty First Dates*. In *Fifty First Dates*, Drew Barrymore's character, suffering from a unique (and fictional) kind of amnesia, wakes up every day, completely forgetting what happened the day before (and all the days before). As a result, she has to relearn who her family is, where she works, and even who she is. To woo her, Adam Sandler's character has to start all over every single day, as though he's meeting her for the first time. He can never rest on the familiarity of history, and it's exhausting.

In *Groundhog Day*, however, Bill Murray's character wakes up every day to the same day with the same people and the same events. After a while, Murray predicts what other people will say and do, allowing him to streamline his day based on what's predictable.

In surgery, we choose the feel of *Groundhog Day* over the feel of *Fifty First Dates* because we want to have a wide range of work to draw on, from the simple to the complicated, the routine to the one for the medical journals. If our work is on a difficulty scale from one to ten and we're always operating (double entendre intended) as though the surgeries lie in the same small range of eight to ten, we'll get bogged down, or, as my dad says, we'll muck around.

A busy surgeon can't take two hours for each of her six hernia surgeries, or she'll never go home. If she treats each case like a complicated one, a ten in difficulty, she'll make things much more intricate than they need to be. Spreading apart the margin of what's easy and what's hard helps her build a body of work to draw on.

There's always a surgeon whose work is forever complicated, requiring intense concentration and time, however. For her, nothing is routine. She believes that no one should treat her surgeries as anything less than serious, energy-draining procedures. She's the one who delays the OR schedule for something that would take the other surgeons half the time and far less intensity. She's stuck on the tough end of the difficulty spectrum, and only she is to blame. In short, she mucks around, treating each case like it's her first, instead of one part of a body of work.

Gut Check

 If you treat everything like it's the most difficult thing you have to do, you'll never get it done. Clear out the clutter to save time and trouble.

DO

Rule Eight: The Enemy of Good Is Better

The hardest part of closing is knowing when you're done. You're tempted to tweak this or shore up that, only to make more work for yourself or, worse, to do real harm. Knowing when good is good enough is the key to finishing up any job.

Every week, I'm waiting to see if I screwed up. All surgeons do it, because if there are any complications, the first few days after the surgery are when they'll hit. Those bad things can be pretty serious, including blood clots, pain, difficulty urinating, partially collapsed lungs, stitches opening back up, internal bleeding, infection, and sepsis, so we close our patients and cross our fingers that nothing bad happens. When there are complications, the surgeon either reoperates or, if nothing can be done, lives with the reality of causing the patient pain or long-term and possibly permanent disability.

Because of this, just before we close the surgery, we might have the urge to try to make something that's good better. We think that if we put in that "midnight stitch," the one that might make sure we don't get called in the middle of the night to treat a surgical complication, we'd sleep better. But then the vessel we touched starts bleeding. That extra cut we made causes a hematoma and needs to be redone, or that bonus stitch creates a tear. Now instead of making a good thing better, we've caused complications.

Here's where the enemy of good is better. You know you did everything right, and it all looks good…but it doesn't look like the drawing in the textbook. Well, it never looks like the textbook! That is best-case-scenario fiction designed to illustrate a procedure.

Drawings don't have cranky tissue or crimping vessels, but your patient does. And in real life, good is good enough.

When it's time to close and call it a day, you have to be okay with giving yourself a B+ or an A–, because in surgery, you just don't get A's. Worse, if you go for the A, you could easily wind up with a D. Settle for good, and you'll sleep better at night.

House Call

 It's getting late, and your report is due in your boss's in-box. You look it over and think it looks quite good. The concepts, the presentation, and the charts all represent your work nicely...except maybe the chart on page thirteen would look better in different colors. Oh, and what if you made it a pie chart instead? So you start futzing around with it, and soon, everything from page thirteen is all messed up. You wind up spending the next hour trying to fix the good that you'd tried to make better. Next time, let it be. Good is good enough!

I'm going to throw my father-in-law under the bus here for a moment, but it's for a good cause, because his experience installing a garage door is a perfect example of better being the enemy of good. My father-in-law is pretty good with tools, but construction is not his trade. A retired businessman, he's more of a weekend tinkerer who takes on home improvements to save a little money and stay out of my mother-in-law's hair. After all, if you can fix it, why not do it yourself?

One weekend, he took on the job of installing a garage door. As home improvements go, this job can be a bit complicated. For starters, garage doors are big and heavy. Some involve a torsion-spring mechanism that puts them under extreme tension and possibly puts the installer in danger. One wrong move, and FWING! You've got heavy-duty springs flying toward you.

My father-in-law did a great job of installing that door. He secured the jambs and the hinges, installed the tracks, affixed rollers and brackets, drilled in the hinges, slid on the door panels, and aligned the track. When he finished, he inspected his work and decided that what he'd done was good, but he thought he could make it a little better if he just added one more screw over heeerre…aaannd…*the entire door fell down.*

"I should have just let it go," he admits. He should have settled for good. He tried to bind it down with straps and cover it up with tarps, but in the end, he called a professional for help, proving that when you're done, you're done. If you try for better when everything is good, it might just all come crashing down on you.

Gut Check

 If you can see a small spot that might improve what you're working on if you just noodle with it a sec, step back. Chances are you're too close to it to see the big picture. Remember, good really is good!

PRINCIPLE FOUR:

DISCHARGE

Is it time for your patient to go home yet, or is she about to have a complication that will send her back to the OR? How do you know when you're done with a patient?

The final D of surgery is Discharge, the part where you and your patient part. You'd think it would be the most straightforward principle, but even Discharge has an art to its science. After all, if everything we did followed strict guidelines, robots could do it. Right now, they can only do parts of it, and those parts are controlled by doctors.

At the end of a case, all is well, or it isn't. Either you've done your job right or you have to explain to the patient and your fellow doctors how and why you haven't. Sometimes you can fix what you've done wrong, but other times, your patients (and you) have to live with your mistakes. Hopefully, you can learn from them so you minimize errors in the future.

Odds are, there will be complications at some point in your career. Patients' bodies are all different, situations are different, and even you are different from day to day. The good news is that the complications have all been reported before, no matter how rare they are. In other words, somebody else has already made the mistakes you may make. You are not alone.

At the end of a case, check with yourself: Did you ask for help when you needed it? Was it the right help, or did that decision cause more harm than good? Is your patient better off because of you? If not, can you live with that, or is there something else you can do?

Discharge is about evaluating both the patient's condition and your work. Chances are, it's all good and everything is better than it was at the start, so here's where you review what you did, so that you can learn from it—the good, the bad, and everything in between. Only then can everyone can go home.

DISCHARGE

Rule One: Be Prepared to Eat Humble Pie

Even the best of us make mistakes, and odds are, you will, too. When it's your turn to eat humble pie, learn to learn from it—instead of blaming and shaming—and it will make you better at what you do.

I can feel the sweat forming on my forehead. I pull out a tissue from the pocket of my white doctor's coat, wipe my brow, take a deep breath, and step onto the stage of the auditorium. In the audience are fifty of my colleagues, their eyes all on me: residents, attendings, fellow surgeons, nurses, and hospital administration big-wigs. On stage is me, just me. Me, and my mistake.

It's the weekly M & M, the morbidity and mortality review committee meeting, where the doctor (or doctors) who made an error that caused major short-term complications, long-term disabilities, or, worst of all, death, presents and reviews what went wrong. In other words, if you messed up, you have to go on stage and tell your peers how you messed up. And believe me, you know exactly how you messed up. That movie's been playing in your head ever since your surgical error hurt your patient, but it won't end until the Department of Surgery grills you about it on stage.

You've been trained to fix your patient's problem, but you didn't do that. Rather, you failed the primary tenet of medicine: *First, do no harm.* Now, your mistake will be with the patient and her family forever.

All surgeons have to deal with this fact, but it never gets easier. The fickle finger of fate will affect every surgeon at some time or another, because nobody and no surgery is perfect. Besides, the odds aren't with you for perfection. For instance, no matter how many colon resections you do, there's a 2 percent leak rate, so for every hundred resections you perform, chances are, you'll have to appear on stage at M & M after two of them.

The surgeon who errs lives with the fact that because of him, his patient suffers. It's an upsetting, guilt-inducing time, and you can't hide from it. The best way to get through it is threefold:

1. Acknowledge the problem.
2. Accept responsibility.
3. Deal with the issue.

Pointing fingers at other people (nurses, residents, and even the patient), doesn't change the fact that you made a mistake. The sooner you deal with it, the better it is for everyone involved, now and in the future.

House Call

 You made a mistake that's going to cost your company thousands of dollars or more. You have to go before the board and give the play-by-play of your mistake. Don't make an even bigger mistake by obfuscating the truth or blaming others. Everyone has to eat humble pie now and then. Accepting that it's a fact of life will help you deal with it.

Read the fine print at the bottom of any professionally researched survey or study and you'll see the "probability of error." Studies are done by humans, so there's a chance for error in every one of them, a probability that can be measured in percentages.

The same goes for medicine. Show me a surgeon who's never made an error in the OR, and I'll show you a surgeon who hasn't

done very many surgeries. Nobody's perfect. Expect mistakes even as you work hard to minimize them, and own up to them when they happen. You can learn from your mistakes only if you identify them. Not learning from your mistakes is a stupid mistake.

Gut Check

 When I was on the basketball court back in college, we had a sportsman-like policy that was almost universally followed. Whenever a player committed a foul, he raised his hand to identify himself. That gesture of responsibility and humility says, "My bad." It's a way of pointing to himself, not at everyone else, and it's a show of respect for the team. After all, nobody's perfect, not even Michael Jordan. When it's your turn to say, "My bad," raise your hand and eat humble pie.

DISCHARGE

Rule Two: Choose Your Help Wisely

Ask for help when you need it, but make sure it's the right help. Consult consultants only when you can't fix the problem yourself, or when trying to fix the problem yourself would cause more troubles.

The surgery was going on ten hours long. Ten hours, when a pair of capable surgeons could have done it in two. The patient was suffering from an aortic aneurysm, a fairly common yet potentially dangerous condition involving a ballooning of parts of the aorta, the body's largest blood vessel. Just about every artery branches off the aorta, so it's a major thoroughfare for life. If an aneurysm ruptures there, it's almost always fatal.

In spite of this, the vascular surgeon believed he could, and should, handle the surgery all by himself. Everything was going fine until, suddenly, a vessel started bleeding. The next thing the surgeon knew, blood was pouring into the iliac arteries, which branch into the pelvis toward each leg. He fixed the artery to the right leg, but the bleeding continued. Then he followed the blood and started to repair another section of the artery. Along the way, however, he managed to injure the bowel and nick the ureter, so he fixed those, too. He searched and fixed, all the while creating more and more complications, which he searched and fixed, hour after hour, in the OR.

At the obligatory M & M confession the following week, a fellow surgeon asked him the question that was on everyone's mind that day: "Why didn't you ask for help?"

Indeed, if he'd asked another surgeon to step in when the first complication arose, he probably wouldn't have been standing in

front of the M & M committee, telling the story about the ten-hour surgery that shouldn't have ended the way it did: with a patient recuperating not just from repairs to his aorta but from damage caused by his own surgeon.

This is why the world's best surgeons often work in tandem for at least part of each surgery. Another set of hands helping out even for ten minutes can prevent complications and bring the surgery to a close more quickly and efficiently. Think about it: If you're hitting a snag, chances are, you'll have a more emotional response to fixing the problem if you're the one who caused it. After all, your pride is at stake, and surgeons can be very proud people—but if you have good help, you can work smarter.

The secret is to walk the line between asking for help from competent coworkers and getting someone else to do the work for you. During the past fifteen years in medicine, I've seen a trend toward outsourcing to consultants. It used to be that an MD handled 90 percent of the medical decisions, turning to specialists only for the remaining 10 percent. Nowadays, however, more and more MDs reach out to consults the moment something specific appears.

For instance, a general practitioner will call in Cardiology for an A-fib, an atrial fibrillation, which is the most common heart rhythm disorder. A patient with an A-fib may feel chest pain, shortness of breath, dizziness, and rapid heart rate. It's identified by EKG or even by taking the patient's pulse, and it's a sign of increased risk for stroke.

But a general practitioner is perfectly capable of running an A-fib's follow-up tests, including an echocardiogram, which is an ultrasound of the heart, or a stress test, and possibly catheterization to check the blood vessels for blockage. An A-fib can be treated by meds or, if needed, cardioversion, an electrical jolt to the heart.

Everything up to this point can be handled by an MD, and yet all too often, a cardiologist will be called in shortly after diagnosis. It's a matter of calling in the consultants too soon, and too often.

When you need help, don't be afraid to ask for it; just make it the right help at the right time.

House Call

 Now you've gone and done it. You completely messed up the birthday cake that one of your customers ordered, and it looks awful. You tried to fix it by mooshing up the icing here and slicing off some of it there, only now it looks worse, and you're too embarrassed to ask your boss, who's decorated cakes for a decade, for help, so you ask the new kid—an actual kid; she's just sixteen—to fix it for you while you occupy your boss elsewhere. She fiddles with the cake for thirty minutes, until finally, it looks way worse than when you'd started decorating it. And the customer just walked in. ... Choose help when you need it, but please choose your help wisely!

When the score is tied up and the minutes are running down on the clock, every basketball player on the court wants to win the game, and win it in regulation time, but your team is being blocked under the net, and the defense looks wary. Going into overtime pretty much means starting over, except with this particular start, everyone's tired and emotions are running high, so the coach puts in a forward with fresh legs and a flair for sinking three-point shots to help the other players on the court finish the job. Sure enough, you score enough baskets to win the game without overtime. No problem.

This is asking for help at its best. The team ran into complications and needed assistance to finish the job of winning the game in regulation time, so a fresh pair of hands with the right stuff came in to help everyone out, with great success.

Calling in consultants, however, is like subbing the entire lineup ten minutes into the game, right when everyone is just getting warmed up. Don't get me wrong; I am not anti-consultant. I mean, I am one! But sometimes when you call in a consultant at the wrong time or for the wrong job, you can actually create more work than is necessary, or you can just plain foul everything up.

I saw it happen in our own surgical department, when the hospital hired consultants to redesign the OR rooms. After the redesign, the overhead lights were in the wrong place and the monitors to see what's going on inside our patients weren't where we needed them to be. If only they hospital had consulted with the people who actually used the equipment, these expensive mistakes wouldn't have happened.

If you're not sure whether you need to ask for help or if consultants are truly necessary for a project, picture yourself at an M & M-kind of meeting, telling your peers and bosses what happened. Are you sorry you didn't ask for help? Or are you sorry you did?

Gut Check

 There's a saying in writing: "Write what you know." Remember this when you consider asking for help. If you know how to do something, you don't really need someone else to swoop in and do it for you, but if you're in over your head, you certainly do.

DISCHARGE

Rule Three: Let Them Go Home

At the tail end of the case is the final decision to let it be. You've done all there is to do, and now it's time to move on, knowing that you used your intuition, facts, gut instincts, education, and experience to reach the end of the process.

The best part about being a surgeon is that when you're done, you're done. Surgery is a mechanical medicine designed to solve a problem for good, not a maintenance medicine in which you try a prescription or protocol and monitor the patient over time. Rather, you go in, fix the problem, and let the patient get on with his life. You clear out the broken appendix, relieve the hernia, or remove the tumor. Then you let your patient go home.

But first, you write up a discharge summary outlining what your patient can expect to experience in the days and weeks post-op, from the required medications to the dietary restrictions to the home care. This is the final formal act between surgeon and patient at the hospital, and it means it's time to move on. It means that you've completed the cycle of surgery: diagnose, decide, do, and now, discharge.

Congratulations. You did your job.

It wasn't easy getting here. On my very first day as a resident, I showed up at six a.m. at a hospital far from my home, where I was handed a stethoscope and sent on rounds for a cardiothoracic surgery rotation. I had to keep up with the chief fellow and the other residents who had months or years of experience, and help them dole out meds to patients, take new-patient histories, discharge post-op patients—all the scut work—for thirty patients over two hours.

I was there to help, but I'm not sure how much I did. It felt like I'd been dropped off in a foreign country where I barely knew the language and didn't know my way around. There was no orientation, no manual. Everything I knew, I'd learned in medical school, but what I needed was practical experience, and the ability to trust my gut that goes along with it.

House Call

 Practice may make perfect, but a cheat sheet gets you there faster. The more you learn about the process of decision making, the better you'll get at it.

It's been said that it takes ten thousand hours for someone to master a skill. Surgeons sock those away during the five-year medical residency, when we learn about evaluating, diagnosing, and operating on patients. With our 110-hour workweeks as residents (nowadays it's a more humane sixty), I hit that 10,000-hour mark near the end of my second year of residency. And yet...

If only I'd been taught the core tenets of how to make good decisions before that, before I was handed my stethoscope and sent out on rounds...

Now that I'm chief of surgery, I see residents coming in fresh from med school, looking as overwhelmed as I so clearly was on day one of my surgical rotation. I see the same decision-making mistakes, and the same problems with diagnosing, deciding, and doing. While it's important that residents learn from their (heavily overseen and corrected) mistakes, it helps when they understand the concepts behind the process, So I teach my residents shortcuts that will help them in the long run, from *determining how sick the patient is* to *calling it how you see it* to *being wary of the easy cases*. When they understand the why behind the how in decision making, they're able to get the job done, and done right, sooner than if they'd waited out their residencies for the secret to success.

Whether you're in charge of helping a gunshot victim who's being wheeled into the ER, or you're up against some other decision, large or small, harrowing or routine, applying the principles of diagnosing, deciding, doing, and discharging will help you make good decisions so you can get done what needs to get done.

So, consider *Trust Your Gut* as your chance to review my detailed and field-tested notes, helping you study for your own board certification and getting you ready for your first rotation at whatever job you do. Now it's time to scrub in, and most of all, trust your gut.